TRAINS

by Lee Sullivan Hill

photographs by Howard Ande

Lerner Publications Company • Minneapolis

To my sister Amy—L. S. H.

To my parents, for spending countless hours trackside nurturing my early love of trains—H. A.

Text copyright © 2003 by Lee Sullivan Hill
Photographs copyright © 2003 by Howard Ande, except as noted on p. 32

This book is available in two editions:
Library binding by Lerner Publications Company, a division of Lerner Publishing Group
Soft cover by First Avenue Editions, an imprint of Lerner Publishing Group
241 First Avenue North
Minneapolis, MN 55401 U.S.A.

Website address: www.lernerbooks.com

Library of Congress Cataloging-in-Publication Data

Hill, Lee Sullivan.
     Trains / by Lee Sullivan Hill ; photographs by Howard Ande.
          p.   cm. — (Pull ahead books)
     Includes index.
     ISBN: 0–8225–0692–0 (lib. bdg. : alk. paper)
     ISBN: 0–8225–0606–8 (pbk. : alk. paper)
     1. Railroads—Trains. I. Title. II. Series. III. Series:
Pull ahead books.
TF147 .H48 2003
385'.2—dc21   2001005912

Manufactured in the United States of America
1 2 3 4 5 6 — JR — 08 07 06 05 04 03

RUMBLE, ROAR. Here comes a train!
What do you see first?

Locomotives lead the way. They pull the train along a track.

Train cars
follow.
CLICKETY-
CLACK.
Can you
count the
cars?

This train has three locomotives and too many cars to count. The cars carry goods like apples and toys. Goods on a train are called **freight.**

Some freight rides inside boxcars. Big doors slide open for loading.

Hopper cars
are loaded
from the
top. These
hoppers
carry coal.

Tanker cars hold liquids like corn syrup.
Tankers look like cans on wheels.

Flatcars are flat. Freight rides on
the top.

Some flatcars carry freight in containers.
Freight containers look like giant boxes.

What kind of freight does this train carry? None! It carries people.

People who ride trains are called
passengers. They get on and off trains
at a railroad station.

Passengers eat in dining cars.

They sleep in sleeper cars.

Coach cars have rows of seats.

Bi-level cars have an upstairs and a downstairs. Can you count the windows?

Trains need people to make them go.
Engineers run the trains. They ride up
high in a cab.

Signals help engineers. These lights
tell which track to follow and how fast
to go.

The engineer does not need to steer. Train wheels fit tightly on the track. The train goes where the track goes.

Trains change tracks to change
direction. **Switches** help trains move
from track to track.

There are many switches and tracks in a train yard. The yard is where trains are put together. Yard locomotives push cars in place.

The cars bump end to end. BAM!
Couplers lock the cars together.

FRED goes on the end of a train. FRED is not a person. It is a Flashing Rear End Device. It tells the engineer if another train is close.

This train is on its way. It will haul
freight across the country.

This train takes passengers to work in a city.

Trains carry goods. They carry people. Are you ready to hop on board?

Facts about Trains

- Railroads have been running in America for 175 years. The first trains were pulled by horses.

- You can ride an Amtrak passenger train in 45 of the 50 states. Many passenger trains carry mail as well as people.

- The Burlington Northern Santa Fe Railroad ships enough sugar each year to make more than three billion batches of cookies!

- Trucks can ride on trains, too. When a truck trailer rides on a flatcar, it's called piggybacking.

- The longest American train was almost 4 miles long. It was made up of more than 500 coal hoppers!

- The longest train in the entire world ran in South Africa in 1989. It had 660 cars and stretched 4½ miles!

Types of Train Cars

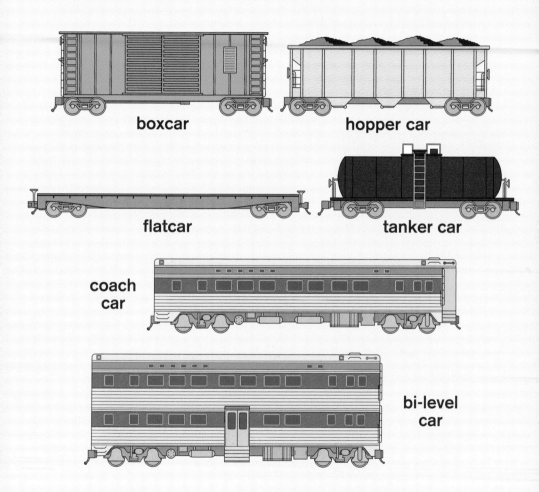

boxcar

hopper car

flatcar

tanker car

coach car

bi-level car

Glossary

couplers: metal pieces that join train cars together

engineers: people who run trains

FRED: a box on the back of a train that tells when another train is nearby

freight: goods that are carried on a train

locomotives: machines that pull trains

passengers: people who ride a train

signals: lights that tell a train where to go and how fast

switches: controls that help a train change tracks

Index

About the Author

Lee Sullivan Hill was lulled to sleep as a child by the low rumble of passing freight trains. When she moved with her husband and sons to Illinois, she found the perfect house beside the Burlington Northern Santa Fe Railroad line. In addition to train watching, Lee enjoys reading, walking, and riding horses. This is her nineteenth book for children.

About the Photographer

Howard Ande has been taking pictures of trains for 25 years. His home is just half a block from a railroad line, so he can walk his dog along the tracks and watch for trains to come by. Besides trains, Howard also takes pictures of factories and beautiful landscapes. He lives in Bartlett, Illinois, with his wife and their two children.

Photo Acknowledgments

Additional photographs courtesy of: © VIA Rail Canada Inc., pp. 14, 15, 16; © Ernest H. Robl, pp. 17, 18; © Kevin Fleming/CORBIS, p. 22. Illustration on p. 29 by Laura Westlund, © Lerner Publications Company.